Playwrights Canada Press is the publishing imprint of:
Playwrights Union of Canada
54 Wolseley Street, 2nd floor, Toronto, Ontario, M5T 1A5
Tel (416) 703-0201; Fax (416) 703-0059
E-mail: cdplays@interlog.com; Internet: www.puc.ca

Playwrights Canada Press operates with the generous assistance of The Canada Council for the Arts—Writing and Publishing Section, and the Ontario Arts Council—Literature Office.

Canadian Cataloguing in Publication Data

Morrissey, Kim, 1955–
    Clever as paint: the Rossettis in love
A play.
ISBN 0-88754-552-1
I. Rossetti, Dante Gabriel, 1828-1882—Drama. 2. Siddal, Elizabeth (1829-1862)—Drama. 3. Morris, William, 1834-1896—Drama. 4. Morris, Jane—Drama. I. Title
PS8576.O7385C53 1998   C812'.54   C98-930155-9
PR9199.3M67C53 1998

Cover: Sharon Broady as Elizabeth Siddal and William Key as Rossetti, in the Hen & Chickens production of *Clever as Paint*, London, England, 1995. Photograph by Barry Shannon. Cover design by Jeremy Scott.

First edition: May 1998. Printed and bound by Hignell Printing, Canada.

August
Bloo

Clever as Paint: The Rossettis in

by
Kim Morrissey

for Gwen,

direct from London

all the best

Kim

Playwrights Canada Press
Toronto • Canada

For Paul

Kim Morrissey's black comedy about Freud, *Dora: A Case of Hysteria* (Nick Hern Books, 1994) is a suggested text for BBC's Open University. She has two published books of poetry: *Batoche* (Coteau Books, 1989) is taught in schools and universities, and five poems from *Poems For Men Who Dream of Lolita* (Coteau Books, 1992) will be reprinted in the Faber and Faber anthology *Mythic Women*. She is currently working on a play about Thomas Chatterton, *this is paradise*, for Dominic Knutton's Cornwall Theatre Collective in Britain.

Author's Note

The playwright would like to thank The Canada Council for the Arts and the Saskatchewan Arts Board for their continued support. She would also like to thank Gareth Edwards, Jan Marsh, and David Rodgers for their careful reading of the various drafts; Michael Gabbay for his technical assistance; curators Richard Price and Leona Carpenter at the British Library for their help and guidance; and Dr. P. R. Nandi (Pain Clinic, National Hospital for Neurology and Neurosurgery, London) for his advice concerning the effects of laudanum and chloral.

Elizabeth Parker's original music is published by BBC World Wide Music, London, WC2B 4PH.

Introduction

Kim Morrissey's *Clever as Paint: The Rossettis in Love* is too wittily subversive to be mistaken for a biographical study. However, its characters are the familiar figures of Pre-Raphaelite mythology: the poet and painter Dante Gabriel Rossetti (1828-1882); his wife and model Lizzie Siddal (1829-1862), herself an artist; and William "Topsy" Morris (1834-1896), poet and craftsman, businessman, and pioneer of practical socialism.

The Pre-Raphaelite world is the canvas of Morrissey's play. In Act One she depicts the relationship of Rossetti and his wife from shortly after their marriage in 1860, to Lizzie's death in 1862; and in Act Two what one might call their "married death," Rossetti's obsession with Siddal in the years 1862 to 1869.

The Pre-Raphaelite woman is an abiding icon in the twentieth century: the static figure in long, jewel-toned medieval dress; her luxuriant hair, large eyes and sensual mouth the focus of the artist's gaze. Pre-Raphaelite paintings of women have been endlessly reproduced, passing into popular consciousness as a type of female beauty. Whether soulful or seductive, the Pre-Raphaelite woman is essentially passive, intro-spective, delivered to the viewer by the intensity of the artist's vision. Lizzie Siddal and Janey Morris were the models for many of Rossetti's most enduring paintings. At various times he drew and painted them both obsessively. They have become types of the Pre-Raphaelite woman, known by Rossetti's depictions, their own identities eclipsed and expropriated by that peculiar fame which attaches to the image rather than the person.

Although the intention of the original Pre-Raphaelite Brotherhood, founded in 1848 by a group of artists including Dante Gabriel Rossetti, John Everett Millais, and William Holman Hunt, was a return to the simplicity of paintings before the time of Raphael, it was also a protest against the formality and what they perceived as the stodginess of contemporary Victorian art. Pre-Raphaelite painting was noted for its insistence on serious subjects, frequently taken from the Bible, Shakespeare, or contemporary poetry. Like many Victorians in an age of rampant commercial development and industrial manufacture, they were drawn to Arthurian legend with its evocation of a lost age of chivalry. The medieval setting and the cult of chivalry lent itself to use of the elaborate symbolism which characterizes Pre-Raphaelite art.

It is perhaps surprising that their output, still popular for what may today be considered its unchallenging content and decorative appeal, was seen by art critics and what we would now call cultural critics as a radical departure, and castigated for its use of bright colour, naturalistic attention to detail, and questionable treatment of subject matter. For example, Dickens savagely attacked Millais' "Christ in the House of His Parents" as blasphemous. However, in 1851 the influential critic John Ruskin came to the defence of the Pre-Raphaelites, and their success was assured.

The original Pre-Raphaelite Brotherhood, whose members never shared a common aesthetic platform, soon dissolved. Rossetti later formed a second wave of the Brotherhood with William Morris and Edward "Ned" Burne-Jones, younger men who met as students at Exeter College, Oxford. They first read Sir Thomas Malory's *Morte d'Arthur* as undergraduates, and from Malory took the chivalric ideals that informed their lives and their art. When they left Oxford in 1856, Morris and Burne-Jones moved to London, where they were drawn to the romantic figure of Rossetti, at this point an established artist and man of the world whose paintings and ideas about art they admired.

Morrissey's first play, *Dora: A Case of Hysteria* (1994), centres on another nineteenth-century cultural icon, Sigmund Freud. Dramatizing his case-study of Dora, Morrissey deconstructs Freud's analysis of the "hysterical woman." The play contrasts Dora's straightforward account of her physical ailments with the distorted edifice constructed by Freud, his diagnosis revealing everything about his own gender and cultural preconceptions, and nothing about the young woman Dora. It is clearly a view of women constructed entirely from the male point of view. The play resonates with twentieth-century parallels. In *Clever as Paint*,

Morrissey similarly gives a voice to the enigmatic Lizzie Siddal, Rossetti's model and wife, and we see how class, gender, and the hierarchies inherent in both the artist/model relationship and in marriage affect Siddal as artist.

Using historical characters promotes a certain duality of vision: the spectator or reader perhaps brings to the play medieval images from Pre-Raphaelite paintings, and may well know the more lurid aspects of the Rossetti marriage and the later Rossetti-Morris *ménage à trois*. The play often upsets our preconceptions. However, events that appear outrageous are usually factual. Rossetti did place the only manuscript copy of his unpublished poems in Lizzie's coffin, and seven years later arranged for her body to be exhumed to retrieve the notebook. After Lizzie's death, Rossetti's passionate involvement with Janey Morris intensified. Their affair became publicly known. Morris protected his wife, leasing jointly with Rossetti a country house, Kelmscott Manor in Oxfordshire, where his wife and her lover could live together. Janey Morris can almost be seen as the fourth character in Morrissey's play: offstage, her story yet to be enacted.

The Art is our starting point: idealized women in a medieval background. Morrissey's depiction of "The Rossettis in Love"—surely an ironic subtitle—cuts across this Pre-Raphaelite ideal. The tension between Art and (fictional) Life is made clear in the staging. In the first scene, Lizzie, while brushing her hair, sings to herself, then assumes a pose which echoes Millais' painting "Ophelia." Siddal had famously modeled for the picture, lying in a tub of water so Millais could paint the effect of water on the fabric of Ophelia's dress. The play begins therefore with the image of a woman posing, *being* someone else as directed by the painter. The power relationship between (male) artist and (female) model is central to the play, present in the dialogue and re-inforced by the recurring tableaux which echo Pre-Raphaelite paintings. This device reverberates: it is not confined to the sphere of Art nor to the Victorian era. The image of woman seen through male eyes is still contested territory.

The real Lizzie Siddal was frequently ill during her long relationship with Rossetti, which had begun in 1851. Marriage was occasionally mentioned, but nothing came of it. Her bouts of illness were never adequately diagnosed. Like many Victorian women, she was treated with the opium derivative laudanum, at the time legally available and medically prescribed. It was the tranquilizer of its day. In 1860, when she and Rossetti had been parted for two years, she became seriously ill. Rossetti joined her in Hastings on the south coast of England, where they married as soon as she was well enough to attend church. It is tempting to see her illness as the body's response to cultural powerlessness, and to recognize in this an aspect of Victorian female invalidism.

Morrissey's Lizzie also struggles against illness. She carries with her the pre-history of her long and fraught relationship with Rossetti. In the play, we see her condition affected by living with Rossetti: his habitual infidelity is hurtful; she humiliates herself, begging for his affection, and threatens suicide when he leaves their studio to teach or visit his family. Her need for Rossetti's love makes her vulnerable and irrational. Yet Morrissey also shows Lizzie the artist, working side by side with Rossetti in easy cameraderie, and winning the praise and patronage of the critic John Ruskin for her poems and drawings. The tension between traditional passive (female) model and active (male) artist is embodied in the character of Lizzie. As artist and poet, she is proud and independent; as model and wife, she is not.

Lizzie's position within the Rossetti family is made awkward by the barriers of social class. She is sensitive to the slights of his mother and sisters, and in two scenes refuses to visit his family. Like nearly all the women who served as Rossetti's models, including Janey Morris and Fanny Cornforth, who became his mistress/housekeeper after Lizzie's death, Siddal came from a lower social class than Rossetti. Her father was a shopkeeper, Janey's a stablehand. Fanny had been a prostitute. Rossetti's father, who had fled Italy as a political refugee, was professor of Italian at King's College, London. The artist/model and male/female hierarchies were reinforced by the male artist's class position.

Morrissey uses Siddal's poems, together with traditional songs, to evoke her inner life. Although Act One ends with Lizzie's death, her ghost is present on stage for much of Act Two. Hers is a thoroughly material spirit, with a fine line in ironic commentary. This element of black comedy frames and qualifies the supernatural aspect of the play. Much of the play's comedy and nearly all its songs and poems are given to Lizzie, lending depth to her character and creating a sense of her strength and potential.

Clever as Paint takes place mainly in the Rossettis' studio. Here domestic and artistic life coincide. At its core, the play deals primarily with the long-disputed relationship between Life and Art. William Morris and Rossetti hold opposing views. Quite unconcerned at his failure to produce a commissioned work, Rossetti argues that Art must be unconstrained: "Art is Art. It justifies itself." Morris's response is baldly practical: a contract has been given, and money has been paid. When Rossetti, with great élan, sidesteps the ethical dimension, we recognize an habitual tactic.

Morris functions as a foil to Rossetti. The real William Morris's reputation, as craftsman and designer, lends weight to the character's aesthetic point of view. Morris's poetry is not widely read today, but in his time it was greatly admired and influenced both William Butler Yeats and Walter de la Mare. His dramatic monologue "The Defence of Guenevere," mentioned in the play, is a free adaptation from Malory's *Morte d'Arthur*. This and other references to Malory evoke the Arthurian legend, with its emphasis on chivalry. The courtly love triangle of Lancelot, Guenevere, and Arthur parallels that of Rossetti, Janey, and Morris. The music of Wagner's *Tristan und Isolde* at the end of the play reinforces this aspect of Morris's relationship with Rossetti. Morris's character is overlaid with the attributes of Arthur/King Marke, the betrayed husband, and Sir Palomydes, the "Great Unkissed." His chivalric restraint and basic decency, in the play and in life, can be seen to parallel his later espousal of practical socialism, where humanitarian concern for the welfare of others is central to his social doctrine.

Rossetti is consistent throughout the play. Sketching Lizzie, he ignores her headache and her need to rest. His "don't move!" cuts across her protests, and abruptly silences her when she confides her desire to bear his child. Personal life is subservient to art. Here as elsewhere, Rossetti's self-centred callousness directs our sympathy toward Lizzie. It is easy to see Rossetti's concern for the primacy of Art as pure egotism.

Early in the play, the contemporary scandal of Byron's affair with his half-sister gives rise to a tortuous piece of reasoning by Morris. He tries to defend Byron, suggesting that if Byron's mother had been unfaithful, the lovers would not have been related. Rossetti sees the speciousness of Morris's argument. The artist's personal morality is irrelevant: "Only the Art matters." Morrissey has established the underlying concern of the play: is the behaviour of the artist—the Life— important, or does Art justify all? Here, because Morris's argument is risible, we may agree with Rossetti. The debate permeates the action, even when it is not articulated in the dialogue. Are Rossetti's infidelities, his affair with Janey Morris, his cavalier attitude to money, his exhumation of Lizzie's corpse to retrieve his poems, relevant? Or are his twin achievements as poet and painter all that matter?

This conflict remains alive throughout the play, largely because Morrissey's skilful characterisation prevents our giving full approval to either man's view. Rossetti is selfish, even ruthless, though his charm is evident. Morris is portrayed as an innocent, a truly good man. His openness and decency make him vulnerable to Rossetti, who in Scene Two commandeers his trousers as lightly as he later appropriates his wife. Near the end of the play, Morris changes sides in the argument, assuring the distraught Rossetti, now terrified of public opinion, that only the Art matters. History prompts us to agree, without excusing Rossetti's behaviour. Yet Morrissey's depiction of Rossetti also makes us question whether a kind of egotism is perhaps intrinsic to the creative process. The play asserts the primacy of Art while undercutting the glamour of the Romantic artist.

Morrissey's theatrical vocabulary is sophisticated. The dialogue is straightforward and lively. Evocative use of music, songs, and poems brings the richness of poetic language to the play. The staging is also assured. The scene where Morris and Lizzie watch Rossetti feed Janey Morris with strawberries is a fine example of clever stagecraft. Rossetti and Janey are offstage, their actions evoked by the words of Morris and Lizzie. We see the lovers through their eyes. With awkward gallantry, Morris and Lizzie imitate the courtship ritual they are watching. Their attempt to define lovemaking as "only pretend" is painful to observe. Spare and precise staging is also used to mark Lizzie's death. Morris lights a candle and begins a traditional part-song, "Man's Life's a Vapour," and Rossetti follows suit. Lizzie, who is dead, lights a candle and joins the round as the third singer. As the round finishes, she is alone on stage. When she finishes the song and blows out her candle, leaving the stage in darkness, the effect is both economical and moving.

Clever as Paint is witty and compassionate. It challenges actors and directors to experiment with the text, play with its variety of means and changes in tone, and explore the complexities of the characters. Morrissey's twentieth-century feminist insights allow us to reconsider the role of the female artist in the context of Victorian social constraints. The playwright's major focus, however, is not gender. Rather, at its core, the play offers an oblique perspective on the process of artistic creation itself.

Beth Chatten

December, 1997
Calgary

Background Chronology

1828:   May 12: Gabriel Charles Dante Rossetti born in London.

1829:   July 25: Elizabeth Eleanor Siddall (later "Siddal") born in Charles Street, Hatten Garden, Holborn. Family originally from Sheffield. (Census information: in 1841, age 11, living at her parents' home, Upper Ground, Southwark; in 1851, age 21, living at her parents' home, 8 Kent Place, no occupation; in 1861, married, age 29 [sic], living at 13 Chatham Place, profession of artist/painter.)

1834:   March 24: William Morris born at Elm House, Walthamstow.

1839:   October 19: Jane Burden born in Helen's Passage, Holywell, Oxford.

1848:   Rossetti helps found the Pre-Raphaelite Brotherhood.

1850:   Siddal sits for several Pre-Raphaelite artists, most notably Rossetti ("Beatrice," 1851) and Millais ("Ophelia," 1852).

1853:   Siddal suffers from ill-health, addicted to laudanum. Morris attends Exeter College, Oxford, planning to take Holy Orders, where he meets Edward "Ned" Jones (later "Burne-Jones").

1855:   Morris meets Rossetti.

1856:   Morris gives up architecture, on the advice of Rossetti, who tells him to be a painter. Siddal is living by herself on Weymouth Street, then moves to Sheffield to take art classes.

1857: Morris and Jones move into Rossetti's old rooms in 17 Red Lion Square. Morris, Rossetti, and others paint the Oxford Union frescoes, and meet Jane "Janey" Burden. In November Rossetti leaves Oxford, with the work unfinished, to stay with Siddal at Matlock Spa.

1858: Spring: Rossetti breaks off engagement to Siddal, and is seen with Ruth Herbert and Fanny Cornforth. He also visits Jane and corresponds with her. Morris publishes *The Defense of Guenevere and Other Poems* and becomes engaged to Jane Burden.

1859: April 26: Morris marries Jane Burden. Commissions Philip Webb to design The Red House, Red House Lane, Upton, as a family home.

1860: April: Rossetti with Siddal in Hastings. May 23: Siddal and Rossetti marry in Hastings and honeymoon in Paris. Mid-May: Janey is pregnant with her first child, "Jenny." The Rossettis return to Blackfriars and combine Numbers 13 and 14 Chatham Place. "Ned" Jones marries "Georgie." June: Fanny Cornforth sits for Rossetti for his painting "Fair Rosamund." Late summer: The Jones and the Rossettis spend most of their time visiting The Red House. Autumn: Siddal is pregnant.

1861: February: Janey gives birth to Jane Alice "Jenny." April: Siddal carries her baby almost to term, but it is stillborn. June: Janey is pregnant with her second child. Morris founds a firm with seven partners (including Rossetti). October: Georgie has her first child, Philip.

1862: February 10, Monday: Siddal takes a fatal dose of laudanum, after a quarrel with Rossetti. He leaves at 9:00pm, finds her unconscious when he returns at 11:00pm. February 11, Tuesday: Siddal dies at 7:20am without regaining consciousness, at the age of 32. The inquest verdict is accidental death. Siddal is buried in Rossetti plot in Highgate Cemetery, Number 5779, with Rossetti's notebook of poems. March 25: Janey's second child, Mary ("May") is born on Lady Day. October: Rossetti moves to Number 16 Cheyne Walk.

1862-69: Rossetti does very little writing. By the mid-1860s he is experimenting with séances. He starts to take chloral as a relief for his insomnia and deteriorating health.

1865: Spring: Janey falls ill, possibly from a miscarriage. Convalesces in Hastings. September: Morris sells The Red House and moves his family, along with the firm, to Queen Square, Bloomsbury (corner of Queen Square and Great Ormond Street).

1868: Rossetti starts to paint Janey Morris regularly. Begins new poems.

1869: October: Rossetti orders Siddal's body exhumed; Charles Howell and others (Rossetti isn't present) retrieve the notebook of poems.

1870: April 25: *Poems by Dante Gabriel Rossetti* (London: F.S. Ellis, 1870) is published. Morris agrees, reluctantly, to review the book, and it is a resounding success.

1871: Morris and Rossetti agree to share the lease on Kelmscott Manor. In October, Robert Buchanan, using the pseudonym "Thomas Maitland," attacks Rossetti's book in *The Contemporary Review*, branding it "the fleshy school of poetry."

1872: June 2: Due to the stress of the controversy over the review and his habitual use of chloral, Rossetti suffers a major nervous collapse. (The usual dose of chloral should be 10-20 grains; Rossetti rarely takes less than a hundred.) His health never recovers.

1882:   Easter Day: Rossetti dies at age 53.

1885:   Morris helps form the Socialist League, and edits the League's journal, *Commonweal*.

1890:   Morris founds Kelmscott Press.

1896:   Kelmscott Press issues *The Works of Geoffrey Chaucer*. October 6: Morris dies at age 62, and is buried at Kelmscott.

1914:   Jane Morris dies at age 75.

My dear Gabriel,

*I will come Tuesday at 3 or half past, though
you did write me such a NASTY LETTER.*

Your affectionate Janey

Undated letter from Janey Morris
to Dante Gabriel Rossetti

Production History

First workshopped by Anabasis Theatre, London, England, in 1994, with the following cast:

ELIZABETH SIDDAL	Eleanor Creed-Miles
GABRIEL ROSSETTI	Simon Hewitt
WILLIAM MORRIS	Aidan James Hurren

First produced at the Hen & Chickens Theatre, London, England, in 1995, with the following cast:

ELIZABETH SIDDAL	Sharon Broady
GABRIEL ROSSETTI	William Key
WILLIAM MORRIS	Steven Dykes

Director: Barry Shannon
Set Design: Miriam Sorrentino and Madeleine Morris
Poster Design: Jeremy Scott
Original Music: Elizabeth Parker

Produced by BBC's Radio Four, and broadcast on December 18, 1997, with the following cast:

ELIZABETH SIDDAL	Imogen Stubbs
GABRIEL ROSSETTI	Paul Rhys
WILLIAM MORRIS	Jonathan Cake
JANEY MORRIS	Alison Pettitt

Director: Cherry Cookson
Original Music: Elizabeth Parker

The Characters

ELIZABETH SIDDAL ("Lizzie")

GABRIEL ROSSETTI

WILLIAM MORRIS ("Topsy")

Act I, Scene 1

*July 25, 1860. The Rossettis' studio:
13-14 Chatham Place, Blackfriars,
London.*

*SIDDAL is brushing her hair, singing
"The Ash Grove" to herself. She hums
first two lines, then sings:*

SIDDAL   "When twilight is fading
I pensively rove
Or at the bright moontide..."

She hums next two lines, then sings:

"With sorrow, deep sorrow
My bosom is laden
All day I go a mourning
In search of my love
Ye echoes, oh tell me
Where is the sweet maiden?
She sleeps 'neath the green turf
Down by the Ash Grove...."

She finishes brushing.

There! I'm respectable!

*Her pose echoes Millais' painting
"Ophelia."*

Act I, Scene 2

1860. The Rossettis' studio.

ROSSETTI, *without trousers, is shaving with his back to* MORRIS *as* MORRIS *enters, so that* ROSSETTI *hears rather than sees him.*

ROSSETTI   William?

MORRIS   Yes.

ROSSETTI   Good! Just in time. Trousers, please. Well, come on! It's past five already! I need your trousers.

MORRIS *starts taking off his paint-splattered trousers.*

(still shaving, still not seeing MORRIS*)* And you can have Lizzie's fob, if you like, next Thursday. Come on, man! Come on! Lizzie's waiting!

MORRIS *solemnly hands his trousers to* ROSSETTI.

ROSSETTI   Bloody fool! You're the wrong William.

MORRIS   Sorry.

ROSSETTI   I can't go to the opera in these. They're disgusting.

MORRIS   Good. Can I have them back?

ROSSETTI   I can't go to the opera without trousers.

ROSSETTI *turns back to shaving.*

MORRIS   I've come for Saint Bartholomew....

ROSSETTI   Not now! Can't you see —

ROSSETTI *cuts himself.*

Damn! Now look what you've made me do! *(pause)* Oh, very well. Since you're here....

ROSSETTI *shuffles through papers and gives* MORRIS *a four-inch watercolour: "Damnation of a Soul to Hell."*

MORRIS   It's lovely. What is it?

ROSSETTI   It's "A Soul Being Carried Down to Hell" — for Lizzie's birthday. But... if you like it, take it. It isn't married to her yet.

MORRIS   It's very good, but....

ROSSETTI   But?

MORRIS   Which one's Bartholomew?

ROSSETTI   *(shrugs)* Which one would you like?

MORRIS   Gabriel. They've commissioned us. It's for Saint Bartholomew's Church. He has to be in the design. He *has* to... he actually *has* to.

ROSSETTI   No, he doesn't.

MORRIS   But they'll be upset if —

ROSSETTI   Good. Art is supposed to upset.

MORRIS   Don't you understand?

ROSSETTI   Art is Art. It justifies itself.

MORRIS	Look, it's not a philosophical debate. It's a commission. If you don't do the work, we have to give the money back.
ROSSETTI	Don't be silly. How can I do that? I've spent it.
MORRIS	You haven't done the work, and you've spent the money. And what am I supposed to tell them?
ROSSETTI	Simple. Tell them it was an advance, not full payment, and ask for double the amount.
MORRIS	Please. Don't joke.
ROSSETTI	I'm not.
MORRIS	We need the money.
ROSSETTI	Money! Money's easy. We can always get money.
MORRIS	If we do the work.
ROSSETTI	Nonsense. I never work, and I've made more money than anyone.
MORRIS	Yes, of course. And that's why you have to borrow trousers to go to the opera, isn't it?
ROSSETTI	Touché! By the way, your Norse saga's over there if you want it. I've finished with it.
MORRIS	Already? It's splendid, isn't it? I think it's splendid. Don't you think it's splendid?
ROSSETTI	I'm sorry. I've tried, but I just can't work up any sympathy for a man who has a dragon for a brother.
MORRIS	*(exploding)* Well, I'd rather have a dragon for a brother than a bloody fool.
ROSSETTI	Topsy! Do you mean *my* brother?

MORRIS	I meant *you*, Gabriel.
ROSSETTI	Surely not! Me, a fool? Who would believe that? Everyone around me marvels at my wit and good-temper.
MORRIS	*(grimly)* Not everyone.
ROSSETTI	Everyone I like.
MORRIS	That isn't very many people.
ROSSETTI	Absolute rubbish. I'm renowned for my circle of friends.
MORRIS	You quarrel with everyone.
ROSSETTI	Never!
MORRIS	Even Janey! And she's a saint!
ROSSETTI	Nonsense. She quarrels with me. It's not the same thing. It's not the same thing at all. Damn. It's past five. He's not coming, is he? Damn.... Hand me your trousers.

ROSSETTI *puts trousers on.*

Thick or thin? Hmm. Thin. Thick takes too long to dry.

ROSSETTI *starts painting over the paint spots on the trousers, using black paint.*

MORRIS	What are you doing?
ROSSETTI	Going to the opera with Lizzie, of course.

Act I, Scene 3

> *Later the same evening.*
>
> SIDDAL *is in bed, vomiting.*

ROSSETTI   You're disgusting. You know that, don't you?

SIDDAL   I'm sorry, I can't help it.

ROSSETTI   You do it deliberately. To humiliate me.

SIDDAL   No!

ROSSETTI   I'm going to the College.

> SIDDAL *makes an affectionate, conciliatory gesture.*

Don't even think of it. And don't even think of apologising. And Swinburne! Chattering all through the opera like some demented fetus.

SIDDAL   I asked him to stop.

ROSSETTI   Like a fish-wife, at the top of your lungs. My God, what did people think, hearing that high-pitched filth coming from both your lips?

SIDDAL   No one noticed.

ROSSETTI   No one!

SIDDAL   You are not, as you believe, the centre of the universe.

ROSSETTI   Neither are you.

	Beat.
SIDDAL	I don't believe there's a class at all.
ROSSETTI	Where am I going, then? Go on. Tell me. Where am I going?
SIDDAL	Why go — why come back with me if you had a class tonight?
ROSSETTI	Someone had to see you home.
SIDDAL	The way you've seen me home all those other times. *(beat)* Please. *(takes ROSSETTI's hand)* You're late already. They've gone home. It's too cold. It's so cold. Please.
ROSSETTI	Lizzie. Don't start. It's too late.
SIDDAL	Please. Just this once. It's my birthday. Please stay. Please.
	They kiss. The tableau resembles ROSSETTI's print "The Kiss."

Act I, Scene 4

	The next morning.
	ROSSETTI *and* SIDDAL *are in bed, sketching each other.* ROSSETTI's *limericks are made up as he speaks.*
ROSSETTI	"There was a young profligate called Georgie Whose life was one continual orgy...."
SIDDAL	*(laughing)* No, no, they have to be true. They're not funny unless they're true!

ROSSETTI	You'd make a beautiful corpse. You'd be lovely, dead!
SIDDAL	I don't want to. I want to be old and ugly and terribly, terribly wrinkled, and alive. Just to see if you could love me for my soul. Could you love me for my soul?
ROSSETTI	"There is a poor creature named Lizzie Whose aspect is meagre and frizzy....'
SIDDAL	I don't like that one very much.
ROSSETTI	"There is a poor creature named Lizzie Whose pictures are dear at a tizzy...." Better?
SIDDAL	How does it end?
ROSSETTI	Badly, I'm afraid. "There is a poor creature named Lizzie Whose pictures are dear at a tizzy And of this the great proof Is that all stand aloof From paying that sum unto Lizzie."
SIDDAL	I'm not just some little shop-girl who dabbles in water-colours. I paint as well as anyone. Better. And I'm a better poet, too.
ROSSETTI	Topsy says your poems are splendid....
SIDDAL	What would he know? Those dreadful old chants... hour after bloody hour....
ROSSETTI	For shame!
SIDDAL	Well, it's hardly entertainment, is it? I told him: "I like a thing perfect." Do you know what he said?
ROSSETTI	"I like a thing done."

SIDDAL	Oh, he's lovely, really. It's just.... You leave me with him all the time. There's no one to talk to.
ROSSETTI	It doesn't matter. No one else talks once he starts, anyway. *(mimics* MORRIS*)* I suppose you're surprised to hear there really is a Greenland Saga. And I suppose you'd expect a Greenland saga to begin: "Once upon a time there was a whale." But it doesn't, as it happens. It begins —
SIDDAL	*(joining in)* It begins: "In olden days Atli sent Knefred to Gunnar...."
ROSSETTI	"To Gunnar." Poor Topsy.
SIDDAL	And why does he let you call him that ridiculous name? He knows you're just laughing at him.... And his poetry! Hour after hour in that "special" rhyming voice.
ROSSETTI	He means well. And he writes quickly.
	"There's an eminent poet named Morris Who all day for his grub swears and worries...."
SIDDAL	It doesn't rhyme.
ROSSETTI	It would for Topsy. All words are equal.
SIDDAL	Oh yes, he's completely democratic, any word will do. If it sounds right, or has the right number of syllables, or might be the sort of word one might use — he does.
ROSSETTI	Well, yes, he's a bit rough. But it's lovely.
	"There was a lady lived in a hall Large in the eyes and slim and tall And ever she sang, against the noon Two Red Roses across the Moon."
SIDDAL	It's lovely, but what does it mean?

ROSSETTI	He's always been a little in love with you, Guggums.
SIDDAL	And Janey. And Georgie, of course. And even your sister Christina. He's in love with everyone. Even that fat trollop, Fanny.
ROSSETTI	Fanny's not fat.
SIDDAL	Say what you will, it's not poetry.
ROSSETTI	Not everyone can write as you do.
SIDDAL	Then they shouldn't write. I don't suffer fools.
ROSSETTI	*(fondly)* I do.

> *Beat.*

SIDDAL	Very clever.... Well, Gug, what do you think?

> *She shows* ROSSETTI *her sketch pad.*

ROSSETTI	*(showing his)* Why Guggums! I look just like you!

Act I, Scene 5

> SIDDAL *is posing.* ROSSETTI *is sketching her.*

ROSSETTI	Don't move!
SIDDAL	No, that's enough. I have a headache.
ROSSETTI	Oh, that's lovely. Just hold your hand there. That's splendid! You make a beautiful corpse. The Lady Elayne, dying for love.

SIDDAL	She didn't die, she just had a baby.
ROSSETTI	No, the other one... pale skin, bright hair, the letter for Launcelot pinned to your breast. Grey-green silk for a shroud.
SIDDAL	Too much like Ophelia. That's enough. You know I have to rest.
ROSSETTI	Just let me finish the cheek. Just one more sketch can't hurt. Just one.
SIDDAL	And what will happen —
ROSSETTI	Don't talk. Please. I'm trying to....
SIDDAL	And what will —
ROSSETTI	Don't move!
SIDDAL	What will happen if I catch cold and die? What will you do then?
ROSSETTI	Finish the lips, of course.
SIDDAL	Don't joke.
ROSSETTI	*(with a great quiet passion)* You know, Lizzie, I'd want to sketch you even if you were dead.
SIDDAL	Your family will be pleased.
ROSSETTI	When I sketch you?
SIDDAL	When I'm dead. Even now, even though — *(realizing)* You haven't told them, have you?
ROSSETTI	I've told them we are married. Of course.
SIDDAL	And... have you told them... it's not just pretend. I want to be a real wife to you... I want a child.

ROSSETTI   Don't move!

SIDDAL   I want a child. I want yours. I want your child,
Gabriel.

ROSSETTI   I said don't move! Stay just as you are! Perfect!

> *Bridewell Church clock starts to strike
> eleven.*

Come on, Dear Dove Divine, time to go.

SIDDAL   I don't want to go. Your sister laughs at me.

ROSSETTI   Maria?

SIDDAL   Christina. And you sit there like a traitor and say
nothing. And whenever you leave the room, she
deliberately ignores me.

ROSSETTI   She's just shy.

SIDDAL   Christina is not shy. And your mother —

ROSSETTI   Oh, what's my poor Mummy done now?

SIDDAL   She treats me as though I'm your wife.

ROSSETTI   But you are....

SIDDAL   Not *just* your wife. As though you were the only
artist in the family. As if I'm nothing, and
you're just pretending I'm an artist to save my
feelings.

ROSSETTI   Don't you see. It's because you *are* an artist.
They don't know what to do with you. They
don't know how to treat you, because....

SIDDAL   Because?

ROSSETTI   Because you're young and beautiful and clever, and an artist and a model and a poet, *and* my wife. Because you're so... so beautifully, terribly, stunningly Lizzie... all the time.

ROSSETTI *and* SIDDAL *kiss.*

SIDDAL   Hulloa, Guggum.

ROSSETTI   Hulloa.

Act I, Scene 6

The Rossettis' studio. Portraits of Fanny Cornforth are mixed with portraits of SIDDAL.

ROSSETTI *is sketching* MORRIS.

ROSSETTI   Keep still!

MORRIS   *(to* ROSSETTI*)* Janey wants to sleep alone. She says I make the bed too hot. That I take the covers and leave her cold. She says I fill up every inch, that I don't leave her room to breathe. That loose hairs on the sheets disgust her. She tells me she would love me if I could change. How can I? She says my bones are too large. She hates the colour of my skin. The way I eat. The way I breathe. The veins under my tongue. She can't bear the way I kiss. The way I trim my beard. She says the sight of me makes her ill.

ROSSETTI   She just finds you too Topsy at the moment. Too loud, too large, too alive, too... too. *Too.* It's tiring, you know, living with a good man. Don't worry. She'll come back to you. Give her time.

MORRIS   But what do I do until then?

ROSSETTI   Be patient. You're her knight, her King Arthur. Tristram to her Iseult.

MORRIS   I feel more like Sir Palomydes.

ROSSETTI   Then you should know all about waiting. She's your Guenevere. Trust her, Topsy. Tell her you trust her.

MORRIS   I can't bear it. She's keeping secrets from me.

ROSSETTI   Secrets! Secrets are nothing. We all keep secrets. It's the truth we can't bear.

> ROSSETTI *passes* MORRIS *a loose page.*

Read her this. Janey likes poetry.

> MORRIS *reads:*

MORRIS   "One face looks out from all his canvasses,
One self-same face sits or walks or leans:
We find her hidden just behind those screens,
The mirror gave back all her loveliness.

A queen in opal or in ruby dress
A nameless girl in freshest summer greens,
A saint, an angel — every canvas means
The same one meaning, neither more nor less.

He feeds upon her face by day and night,
And she with true kind eyes looks back on him,
Fair as the moon and joyful as the light.
Not wan with waiting, nor with sorrow dim;

Not as she is, but was when hope shone bright;
Not as she is, but when she fills his dream."

ROSSETTI   Good, isn't it?

MORRIS   Is it yours, or Lizzie's?

ROSSETTI   Christina's, actually.

MORRIS   And why is it called "Christmas Eve?"

ROSSETTI   It was a gift.

MORRIS   It's very good.

ROSSETTI   She'll be so pleased. I'm seeing her tomorrow.
                She wants to paint. I said "no" of course. One
                artist in the family is enough.

MORRIS   What about Lizzie? That's two.

ROSSETTI   One Rossetti is enough.

MORRIS   Oh....

ROSSETTI   You treat your wife the same way.

MORRIS   Nonsense. I let Janey do anything she likes.

ROSSETTI   So long as it's tapestry.

MORRIS   *(hurt)* Embroidery as well.... I love watching her
                sew. Like some sad medieval maiden, "waiting...
                but not for me."

ROSSETTI   Janey hates it. She says it hurts her back.

MORRIS   Balderdash. When did she say that?

ROSSETTI   And it hurts her eyes. She's worried about going
                blind.

MORRIS   Honest work never hurt anyone.

ROSSETTI   And it gives her wrinkles.

MORRIS   She's more perfect and more beautiful than the
                first day I met her.

ROSSETTI   *I* met her.

MORRIS	"A saint! An angel! Every canvas means the same one meaning...." That's very nice. I suppose your sister wrote it for Lizzie.
ROSSETTI	I don't think so. I think she may have written it for you.
MORRIS	Ah. Now that's exactly my point. How can we tell, with Art? Which brings us back to the question. If the rumours are not entirely untrue, it might not be impossible to suppose — that hand's too large, by the way.
ROSSETTI	Oh, get to the point!
MORRIS	Well, don't you see, if it is their *father* they share, and not their mothers —
ROSSETTI	They'd only burn in hell for half an eternity.
MORRIS	No. It might just appear to be incest. If his mother lied, which meant his father was not his father, or *her* father *her* father, then one might see how — it might justify, it would certainly explain why they —
ROSSETTI	You're disgusting.
MORRIS	It's not me — Why? What have I said? What's wrong?
ROSSETTI	My God. You don't mind having a dragon for a brother, but you object to straight-forward sex. If Byron fucked his sister, he fucked his sister. It doesn't affect the poems in any way. Only the Art matters.

ROSSETTI *throws down his brush.*

That's enough, Tops.

MORRIS	I can stay another hour.

ROSSETTI   No. I'm taking tea alone with Fanny.

MORRIS   Gabriel. For shame. What must Lizzie think!

ROSSETTI   Lizzie doesn't know.

MORRIS   Everyone knows. Even I know, and I never know
                  anything. Even Janey thinks you're appalling.

ROSSETTI   Janey — never!

MORRIS   I know my own wife. She's disgusted at the
                  thought of her in your bed.

ROSSETTI   Ah. Well, if that's all, tell her it's not just the
                  bed. Fanny stands on the wash-basin as well.

Act I, Scene 7

                  The Rossettis' studio.

                  SIDDAL *is brushing her hair, singing
                  "Early One Morning."*

SIDDAL   "Oh don't deceive me
                  Oh never leave me
                  How could you use a poor maiden so?"

                  She finishes brushing.

                  There. I'm respectable.

                  *Her pose echoes Rossetti's painting
                  "Beata Beatrix."*

ROSSETTI   Good.

                  ROSSETTI *is getting his paint brushes
                  ready.*

SIDDAL	I don't want to go.
ROSSETTI	Don't go then. Ruskin can wait.
SIDDAL	I have to. We need the money.
ROSSETTI	And he likes lovely young things.
SIDDAL	I'm not young.
ROSSETTI	You're still lovely.
SIDDAL	*(dryly)* Not according to Mr. Ruskin.
ROSSETTI	So much the better. You've found a man who loves you only for your soul.
SIDDAL	And my Art.
ROSSETTI	Exactly. And *we* love *him* for his money. So bring back loads of tin. Loads and loads of tin.
SIDDAL	Come with me.
ROSSETTI	No. It's you he wants. He's *your* patron now, not mine, thank God.
SIDDAL	You're very rude to Mr. Ruskin. He says you don't respect him.
ROSSETTI	It's not me. It's him. Idiot.
SIDDAL	And you'll be here when I return?
ROSSETTI	*(teasing)* Perhaps. Of course. Topsy's coming.
SIDDAL	For tea?
ROSSETTI	No. With Fanny.

Silence.

Topsy's "Saint Peter" for the new St.
Bartholomew.

SIDDAL   And Fanny?

ROSSETTI   "Mary Magdalene," of course.

SIDDAL   I have such a headache. Perhaps I should stay.

ROSSETTI   It's only twice a year… think of the money.
Wait! Will you read?

They examine SIDDAL's pages.

SIDDAL   I thought "When We Met Ourselves," or perhaps
this to go with this? *(shows sketch)*

ROSSETTI   No, he hates ghosts. Read this. He likes fair
ladies dying of love. Unless they're his wife.
Yes, perfect! Let's hear it… just to be sure.

She recites, hesitantly:

SIDDAL   "Oh never weep for love that's dead
For love is seldom true…."

ROSSETTI   More feeling. And speak up. His drawing room
is enormous. And if he asks, remember: I'm very
poor — but too proud to ask. And if he doesn't,
mention the Brownings. Now, begin again:
(thrillingly) "Oh never weep for one that's
dead…."

SIDDAL   "Oh never weep for one that's dead…."

ROSSETTI   Much better!

Act I, Scene 8

Split scene tableaux.

Tableau: SIDDAL *is hesitantly reciting at Ruskin's house, Herne Hill.*

SIDDAL "Oh never weep for love that's dead
For love is seldom true
But changes his fashion from blue to red
From brightest red to blue
And love was born to an early grave
And is so seldom true...."

SIDDAL *continues, with confidence.*

"Then harbour no smile on your bonny face
To win the deepest sigh
The fairest words on truest lips
Pass on and sweetly die
And you will stand alone, my dear
When wintry winds draw nigh...."

Tableau: MORRIS *outside, knocking on* ROSSETTI's *door.*

MORRIS Are you there? Have I come too late? Gabriel...
Gabriel... can you hear me? I can hear you. Let
me in! Gabriel? Are you there, Gabriel? It's
Topsy... Gabriel... let me in....

Tableau: SIDDAL, *confident, shimmering, ethereal.*

SIDDAL   "Sweet, never weep for what cannot be
                For this God has not given
                If the merest dream of love were true
                Then sweet, we should be in heaven
                And this is only earth, my dear
                Where true love is not given...."

                            Blackout.

Act I, Scene 9

                    Later the same day.

                    ROSSETTI *stands without trousers,*
                    back turned, washing Fanny's menstrual
                    blood off his penis and pubic hair.
                    Painting of Fanny is on the easel.

SIDDAL   *(bursting in)* Gug! Look! Loads of tin. Loads and
                loads of tin! And Mr. Ruskin says —

ROSSETTI   *(still washing)* You're back early.

SIDDAL   He says I'm reminiscent of Blake! Of Blake!
                (pause) And — what are you doing?

ROSSETTI   Nothing. Washing. Go on.

SIDDAL   And he told me what's wrong with you: He said
                you're lazy, thinking only of what you like and
                don't like, instead of what would be kind. He
                says I'm better! The plain hard fact of it, Mr.
                Ruskin said, is that I have genius. Genius! Me!
                And then he said as a genius I must find someone
                noble to love and trust, and then count no
                sacrifice too great to make in that one's service.
                And I said I had!

SIDDAL *embraces* ROSSETTI *from behind.*

ROSSETTI Mmm. Good.

SIDDAL *(looking down)* Oh, you've cut yourself! You're bleeding! Have you cut yourself? Show Guggum where, poor, poor!

ROSSETTI Go away.

SIDDAL But the water's all — *(pause)* You traitor. You... traitor.

ROSSETTI Very eloquent, Guggum.

SIDDAL How dare you... how dare you do this to me in my own home? How dare you? You... you....

ROSSETTI Traitor?

SIDDAL *slaps* ROSSETTI's *face.*

Act I, Scene 10

Several days later.

SIDDAL *is reciting, bitterly, to* ROSSETTI, *who is eating an apple.*

SIDDAL "Ope not thy lips, thou foolish one
Nor turn to me thy face;
The blasts of heaven shall strike thee down
'Ere I will give you grace.

Take thou thy shadow from my path
Nor turn to me and pray
The wild wild winds thy dirge shall sing
'Ere I will bid thee stay.

> Turn thou away thy false dark eyes
> Nor gaze upon my face
> Great love I bore thee; now great hate
> Sits grimly in its place.
>
> All changes pass me like a dream
> I neither sing nor pray
> And thou art like the poisonous tree
> That stole my life away."

ROSSETTI   Mmm. It's lovely. I don't think "ope" works entirely... and I don't like "Great love I bore thee" — never invite the reader to be bored with anything. The ending's splendid, though. Blake. You meant that, didn't you. Do you have a title? It's always useful to have a title. It focuses the poem. "Love or Hate".... No! "Love *and* Hate." Yes. Better. Much better.

        Bridewell Church clock strikes eleven.

        Time to go.

SIDDAL   I don't want to go. And if you loved me —

ROSSETTI   I love you. And I'm going. I have to go — they're my family.

SIDDAL   No! Don't leave me! I'll die if you leave me!

ROSSETTI   They're my family.

SIDDAL   Then go. Go. And I'll go, too. One drop for every minute you're away.

ROSSETTI   It's only two hours.

SIDDAL   Good. That should be just about enough, shouldn't it? One hundred and twenty.

ROSSETTI   Really? I'd take all the laudanum in the room if I were you. If a thing's worth doing, it's worth doing well.

ROSSETTI *exits, slamming door.*

SIDDAL You're *not* me.

You take everything.

I'm your family. Me.

Good. Go. Do whatever you please. Please
yourself. And I will, too. I'll behave as badly as
you, Gug. Worse, if I choose. Worse.

Act I, Scene 11

*September, 1860. Picnic at the Red
House, Bexley Heath, Kent — the
MORRIS house.*

*SIDDAL is watching Janey Morris and
ROSSETTI flirt at the picnic. SIDDAL
has just found out she is pregnant.
MORRIS is showing SIDDAL yet
another medieval book.*

MORRIS And look at this! Look at the vellum! That's
first-rate, that is!

*MORRIS has been showing her his
books for a very long time....*

SIDDAL Yes, they're lovely....

MORRIS The old books are the best! And the colour, even
now, five-hundred years later. That's the sort of
thing I want to do. If I can. Work that will last.

SIDDAL It's beautiful. Can I have it?

MORRIS *(dismayed)* If you like.

SIDDAL	Oh, William. It was only a joke!
MORRIS	No, please. Take it.
SIDDAL	You're such a darling. There's nobody like you on this earth. There isn't anybody who *exists* that in the least *bit* resembles you.
MORRIS	Dear Lizzie, you're quite splendid, you know. We all love you.
SIDDAL	Thank you.
MORRIS	It isn't just me. Janey adores you.

Beat.

	Is anything the matter? Is there anything I can get you? Anything I can do?
SIDDAL	Thank you. No.
MORRIS	I'm sorry. He's always like this, when he's with Janey. It's just pretend.
SIDDAL	But why does he have to feed her strawberries?
MORRIS	It's August. They're in season.
SIDDAL	It's September. And to lick the cream off before he gives them.... It's disgusting. And why does he have to sit at her feet?
MORRIS	They all do it, you know. Not just him. She expects it.
SIDDAL	Well, she shouldn't. It's too much.
MORRIS	It's a wonder Janey can eat them. She's... you know.
SIDDAL	She's not the only one.
MORRIS	No one said.

SIDDAL	Why do you think I've been so ill?
MORRIS	We were afraid... after last spring.... I'm so pleased. *(cheerfully)* Damn me. Have a strawberry.
SIDDAL	Is that the way you hand them to your wife? No wonder she prefers my husband.
MORRIS	I'm sorry... of course not... of course. *Beat.* A strawberry, dear lady?

SIDDAL	Why, thank you, kind sir. But wait.
	
	          SIDDAL *bites into it, then offers*
	          remaining half to MORRIS.
	
	The same again to you, sweet knight.

MORRIS	With pleasure. Another, milady?
SIDDAL	From my lips to yours.
MORRIS	You see — it's just pretend.
SIDDAL	It's great fun — to pretend — isn't it?
MORRIS	I love her. I can't paint her, but I love her. And Gabriel can. That's all there is to it.
SIDDAL	I'm sorry. When I saw them together, I thought.... I'm sorry.
MORRIS	I know you talk to Janey. What does she want? What does Janey want? You're a woman. What do *you* want?
SIDDAL	More strawberries, Topsy. More strawberries.

Act I, Scene 12

November, 1860. The Rossettis' studio.

MORRIS and SIDDAL are examining a stack of medieval books. ROSSETTI enters.

ROSSETTI   Hulloa! What are you doing with my wife!

SIDDAL   Waiting for you, of course. William's been showing me his new books.

ROSSETTI   Complete with worms! Have you seen any of Southey's Cottonilia?

MORRIS   Yes, I saw one just yesterday. Disgusting.

SIDDAL   One of his own books?

MORRIS   No, that was the worst of it. It wasn't. It was White of Selborne. "Works On Natural History"... volume one. Not a great beauty at any time.... But in cotton!

SIDDAL   But what's the harm, if it's clean and respectable?

MORRIS   You lose the smell of the leather, and the way the eye rests on the edges. Green labels, India ink, aniline dye! It hurt my teeth just to look at it!

SIDDAL   But surely a book you can use is better than some ragged old worm-eaten thing that comes away at your touch.

MORRIS	No, it's not.
SIDDAL	What do you think, Gug?
ROSSETTI	I agree with Topsy, Guggum. Books aren't just for reading.
MORRIS	They're not for reading at all.
ROSSETTI	Ah. There we disagree.
MORRIS	No. You're right. They're for reading, but they're also for the pleasure of their company. Like a pipe, or a good piece of silk. Useful, but beautiful in themselves. Cotton is too light. And it was the wrong blue altogether. And the wrong weight. A book has to weigh something if it's to mean anything at all.
ROSSETTI	Oh, Topsy! You must be the only man alive who would weigh a book first, to decide how good it is.
MORRIS	Yes, yes I would. Everything should take up the proper space.
ROSSETTI	I don't give a damn about space. Only the words matter.
SIDDAL	*(to* ROSSETTI*)* But what about blank books? Don't *they* have an obligation to be beautiful?
ROSSETTI	All I need is a sketch-pad.
SIDDAL	What a pity. It means you won't be needing this....

MORRIS *brings out gift notebook.*

	It's a surprise!
MORRIS	Sorry about the colour...

SIDDAL	No, it's lovely!
ROSSETTI	It's exactly right.
MORRIS	...looks like wet mould on a corpse.
SIDDAL	It's Elayne, dying of love!
ROSSETTI	*(opens it)* It's blank.
SIDDAL	*(to* ROSSETTI*)* Yes! It's for you. For your poems. To keep them safe. So when this book is finished, your book will be finished as well.
MORRIS	And Lizzie promises to fair copy whatever you like, whenever you like, without changing it —

ROSSETTI *and* SIDDAL*'s shared joke.*
SIDDAL *always changes his lines.*

ROSSETTI	(together) Much.
SIDDAL	(together) Much.
ROSSETTI	Hand me your pencil, Tops.

ROSSETTI *writes on the fly leaf.*

MORRIS	What, a poem already!
ROSSETTI	A dedication.
SIDDAL	*(reads)* "Guggum. Her Book." But it's yours! It's for you!
ROSSETTI	Ah. But all my poems are for you.

Act I, Scene 13

Christmas, 1860. The Rossettis' studio.

Medieval Christmas music. ROSSETTI *is dictating to* SIDDAL.

ROSSETTI "Her eyes knew more of rest and shade
Than a deep water even...."

(a new thought) No!

"Her eyes know more of rest and shade
Than waters still'd at even...."

No, strike that out.

SIDDAL I haven't written it. "Fair copy" means perfect.

ROSSETTI *(musing)* "Her eyes were deeper than the depth
Of waters still'd at even...."

"Her blue eyes...."

SIDDAL My eyes aren't blue.

ROSSETTI You're breaking the mood!

SIDDAL I don't like that one very much. Is there anything else you'd like copied? Something perfect.

ROSSETTI No. Yes. If you insist.

"Lazy, languid, fair-haired... Jenny..."

Comma.

"Fond of a drink and fond of a guinea..."

Comma.

"Whose head upon my lap you keep — "

> SIDDAL *throws book at him. Starts to pack a hold-all.*

You're not writing! What's wrong? It's only a poem.... Can't you see how important this is? No one has ever done this — no one has ever treated women like her —

SIDDAL   Trollops.

ROSSETTI   — in quite this way before. Can't you see, it's a sermon. It's my best poem... it's my *only* poem... What does it matter who it's written to...?

SIDDAL   It's written to Fanny.

ROSSETTI   No one will know. I've changed the name. Can't you see — it's the best thing I've done.

SIDDAL   These are my poems. For me. They should be written for me.

ROSSETTI   Very well. "Lazy, languid, fair-haired Lizzie...."

> SIDDAL *starts to exit.*

Go on, then. I don't care.

SIDDAL   Mr. Ruskin says —

ROSSETTI   Ruskin! What does he know? He said "Jenny" doesn't rhyme with "guinea." I told him "eye" didn't rhyme with "symmetry" either. Idiot.

Beat.

(shouts) Don't come back. Do you hear? And don't write. I won't answer. I won't even open it. I won't read anything you have to say, ever, if you leave!

SIDDAL   Good!

Door slams.

Act I, Scene 14

The next day. The Rossettis' studio.

ROSSETTI   Women! Selfish, lying, unscrupulous bitches, every one.

MORRIS   Gabriel, where's Lizzie?

ROSSETTI *shows* MORRIS *a portrait of Fanny.*

ROSSETTI   I've finished Fanny's "Mary Magdalene." What do you think of her eyes?

MORRIS   Too blue.

ROSSETTI   Hmm. What do you think of her mouth?

MORRIS   Too large.

ROSSETTI   Really?

MORRIS   Yes.

ROSSETTI   Good. I thought it was too small, but if you think it's too large... it must be exactly right.

MORRIS	That red lead for flesh won't last, you know.
ROSSETTI	But it's lovely, isn't it?
MORRIS	It will go black in your lifetime.
ROSSETTI	I don't intend to live that long.

Beat.

MORRIS	Don't worry. She'll come back.
ROSSETTI	Do you really think so?
MORRIS	It's Christmas. She's with child. Where could she go?

Act I, Scene 15

April, 1861, 2:00am.

SIDDAL *is painting furiously. She is eight months pregnant.*

SIDDAL	*(to herself)* I can't... I can't! *(to* ROSSETTI*)* Go away!... I can't. I just can't.
ROSSETTI	It doesn't matter. Ruskin can wait. Come back to bed. It doesn't matter.
SIDDAL	But it does! We need the money, Gabriel. We need the money. And with the baby coming... and I can't... I can't... I can't breathe for the worry. It's like an iron band, pressing down. I can't breathe!
ROSSETTI	Let me see. Here....

SIDDAL　　　　　No. It's *my* work Mr. Ruskin wants. Mine. Me.

ROSSETTI　　　　But, Lizzie....

SIDDAL　　　　　Me. He wants me.

ROSSETTI　　　　But you do it for me, why can't I do it for you?
　　　　　　　　　　No one will know.

SIDDAL　　　　　I want it to be mine, completely mine. My own.
　　　　　　　　　　I want to make my own name.

ROSSETTI　　　　But why not do it together? No one can tell.
　　　　　　　　　　We'll be the sort of people poor old Topsy wants
　　　　　　　　　　everyone to be. Equals. Not pupil and teacher, or
　　　　　　　　　　disciple and mentor, or husband and wife. Equals.
　　　　　　　　　　We'll do it together — tomorrow. Just come to
　　　　　　　　　　bed. You're so cold... please.... Please. Think of
　　　　　　　　　　the baby.

SIDDAL　　　　　That's all I think of. I can't feel it. I haven't felt
　　　　　　　　　　it for weeks, and I'm so afraid. I can't feel
　　　　　　　　　　anything.

ROSSETTI　　　　Come to bed. It will be better in the morning.
　　　　　　　　　　And soon we'll have a beautiful, beautiful child,
　　　　　　　　　　born on my birthday, who looks exactly like his
　　　　　　　　　　mother.

SIDDAL　　　　　Her mother.

ROSSETTI　　　　My mother.

SIDDAL　　　　　Mine.

Act I, Scene 16

May, 1861. A week after SIDDAL*'s miscarriage.*

SIDDAL *is singing her poem "Lord May I Come," as a lullaby.*

SIDDAL

"How is it in the unknown land?
Do the dead walk hand in hand
God give me trust in thee.

Do we clasp dead hands and quiver
With an endless joy forever?
Do tall white angels gaze and wend
Along the banks where lilies bend?
Lord we know not how this may be:
Good Lord we put our faith in thee
O God, remember me...."

MORRIS

(calling) Hulloa!

SIDDAL

(calling) Hush, Georgie! Don't wake the baby!

ROSSETTI

(calling) It's not Georgie — it's Tops.

MORRIS

(to ROSSETTI*)* But why is she — ?

ROSSETTI

It's pretend. It's just pretend. I'm sure it's just pretend.

SIDDAL

"Do we clasp dead hands and quiver
With an endless joy forever..."

MORRIS

It's a little morbid.

ROSSETTI	She's a poet.
MORRIS	How long has she been… pretending…?
ROSSETTI	A week, maybe two. She died in my arms after the birth, you know. She was dead, and I said "Breathe!" And she did! She came back for me.
MORRIS	And the baby? Howell said it was —
ROSSETTI	It was nothing. Rotting. Rotting for weeks. Poor Lizzie, so proper, and all the time to have that… thing… rotting inside her. I told Fanny —
MORRIS	How could you? If you loved Lizzie —
ROSSETTI	Don't you understand anything? It's *because* I love Lizzie. I love her, but I have to be with someone. Physically *be* with someone. Anyone. I can't bear being alone.
MORRIS	Then be with me. Stay with us. Come to the Red House. The country air will do you good.
ROSSETTI	I can't leave Lizzie.
MORRIS	I meant the both of you. Spend the summer, if you like.
ROSSETTI	But what would Janey say?
MORRIS	She's my wife. She'll say yes.

Act I, Scene 17

Christmas, 1861.

Christmas music: "God Rest Ye Merry Gentlemen." MORRIS *is looking at a sketch of Janey.*

MORRIS   Now, that's nice. That's very nice. When did you do that?

ROSSETTI   Look at the way the line of the throat echoes the line of the hand. "J" for Janey. Clever, isn't it?

MORRIS   It's a lovely thing. And, of course, Lizzie must be pleased.

ROSSETTI   Lizzie? Why?

MORRIS   Well, if you're painting Janey, you're not... painting... Fanny. And, of course, with Janey, there's no question....

ROSSETTI   No question at all.

MORRIS   My God, that's good! That's very nice. I wish I could paint. If only I had learned to draw.

ROSSETTI   It's not drawing you need. It's intelligence. That's what makes Lizzie so wonderful. She's so... clever. When I see her there... seeing her so ill, and knowing — I can't bear seeing her so pale and thin and beautiful....

MORRIS   Then why torment her?

ROSSETTI   I don't.

MORRIS	Quite frankly, you can either act like a damned scoundrel, or you can.... Life isn't Art, Gabriel.
ROSSETTI	Art is all the Life we need.
MORRIS	Oh, nonsense. And a good thing, too. You're the laziest artist I know!
ROSSETTI	Don't be silly. Ned is.
MORRIS	Ned! Ned works from nine to nine!
ROSSETTI	There. You see! He's so lazy, once he's sat down, he's too lazy to get up again. "There was a young painter called Jones Whose conduct no genius atones...."
MORRIS	You're no better. We just can't find a rhyme for "Rossetti."
SIDDAL	*(sleepily)* Is that William? Have you eaten? Shall we go down to the Green Dragon?
ROSSETTI	Go back to sleep, Gug. Topsy can look after himself.

Act I, Scene 18

February 10, 1862. 9:00pm.

ROSSETTI is revising a love poem. The poem isn't about SIDDAL. SIDDAL hovers.

ROSSETTI	*(to SIDDAL)* Go away!
SIDDAL	Please... please... I feel so cold.

ROSSETTI   And don't even think of apologizing.

SIDDAL   If I could just get warm... just under your arm...
just there... yes... I like this.... *(puts her head in
his lap)* Shall we go to bed now?

ROSSETTI   I'm going to the College.

SIDDAL   Oh, let's not quarrel. Please... think of the baby.

ROSSETTI   I have to teach.

SIDDAL   I said I don't care, God damn you!.... Oh,
please... please, I'm sorry... I'm so sorry...
please... just come to bed... or take me. Draw
me. Draw me any way you like. Do anything
you like... if you like. Yes, take me! I'll be your
Guggum....

SIDDAL *poses.*

Your Goddess... your Madonna With Child...
your Whore.... Is this what you like? Is this
what Fanny does?

ROSSETTI   You'll catch cold.

SIDDAL   Is this why you prefer her to me?

ROSSETTI   Stop it.

SIDDAL   I swear, I swear, if you leave, you'll kill me. If
you leave me, I'll —

ROSSETTI   Will you be quiet!

SIDDAL   You make me so miserable, I don't care any
more. I want to be dead.

ROSSETTI   Good. It would be a blessing.

SIDDAL	Please. Please... I love you. I love you, Guggum. Please.
ROSSETTI	I have to go. I have to teach.
SIDDAL	Where are you really going? You can tell me. It doesn't matter.
ROSSETTI	Out. I'm going out. Alright?
SIDDAL	Then go. And I'll go, too. One drop for every minute you're away.
ROSSETTI	I'll be back in two hours.
SIDDAL	Good. That should be just enough time, shouldn't it? And if it doesn't kill me, let's see what it does to the baby. Shall we see if we can kill this one the way we killed the last?
ROSSETTI	I don't give a damn about the baby. Drink the whole bloody lot for all I care. And good riddance.
SIDDAL	But why can't I come? Why not? Tell me why. Because you're going to *her*.
ROSSETTI	No. Because I can't stand the smell of you.

ROSSETTI *exits.*

SIDDAL *collects and sorts through her papers, drinking laudanum.*

SIDDAL	"Oh never weep for one who's dead For love is seldom true...."

She puts the poem in a pile with others, then picks up another.

"When I am dead my dearest
Sing no sad songs for me
Lay thou no flowers at my grave...."

> *Crumples it up, then picks up another.*

"Not wan with waiting, nor with sorrow dim...."

> *Crumples it up, then picks up another.*

"Lazy, languid, laughing Fanny...."

> *Crumples it up.*

My life is so miserable
I wish for no more of it
My life is so miserable....

> *Picks up "Jenny" poem, and writes on other side:*

"My life
Is so miserable
I wish for no more of it."

> SIDDAL *scatters all the papers, except for her note, and drinks the laudanum left in the bottle.*

> *Her pose echoes* ROSSETTI's *"Beata Beatrix" painting.*

Act I, Scene 19

>ROSSETTI *is putting a glass to*
>SIDDAL*'s lips, to check for breath.*

ROSSETTI   *(to* SIDDAL) Breathe!

MORRIS   *(to* ROSSETTI) It's a smudge on the glass. Just a smudge.

ROSSETTI   Perhaps the drug just slowed her heart, and she just seems —

MORRIS   Gabriel. I'm sorry. She's gone.

ROSSETTI   *(to* SIDDAL)You died for me. You died for love of me. And now all my poems will stay with you. Just there. Guggum. Your book. Under your clever little head. Fair copy. To keep safe. Forever.

>*Beat.*

>MORRIS *sings "Man's Life's a Vapour," a traditional folk song.*

MORRIS   "Man's life's a vapour full of woes
He cuts a caper and down he goes
Down and down and down and down
And down he goes...."

>*Beat.* MORRIS *lights a candle, and starts the round.*

"Man's life's a vapour full of woes..."

ROSSETTI *lights a candle, and joins the round.*

ROSSETTI   "Man's life's a vapour full of woes..."

They complete the round. The second time through, SIDDAL *lights a candle and joins the round as a third singer.*

SIDDAL   "Man's life's a vapour full of woes..."

The round is lead three times by MORRIS. *At the end, each singer blows out his candle when he finishes singing, until it is only* SIDDAL *who is lit with a candle.* SIDDAL *sings alone:*

"Down and down and down and down and down she goes...."

SIDDAL *blows out candle.*

Blackout.

End of Act 1

Act II, Scene 1

ROSSETTI *and ghostly* SIDDAL *recite
"The Unquiet Grave," a traditional folk
song.*

ROSSETTI

"Cold blows the wind to my true love
And gently falls the rain
I only had but one true love
And in greenwood she lies slain
I'll do as much for my true love
As any young man may;
I'll sit and mourn all on her grave
A twelve month and a day.

When the twelve month and one day was passed
The ghost began to speak:
Why sittest here all on my grave
and will not let me sleep?
There is one thing that I want, sweetheart
one thing that I crave,
and that is a kiss from your lily white lips,
then I'll go from your grave...."

SIDDAL

"Oh, my lips they are as cold as clay
my breath smells earthy strong
and if you kiss these cold clay lips
your days will not be long...."

Act II, Scene 2

> *July 25, 1869.* ROSSETTI'*s studio at 16 Cheyne Walk, Chelsea, London.*
>
> *Sketches and paintings of "Beata Beatrix" are everywhere.* ROSSETTI *is seated at a table.*

MORRIS   Sorry I'm late. I've been showing Janey how to dye.

ROSSETTI   Is she all right?

MORRIS   Yes, of course. The floor's a bit of a mess, but the silk looks lovely. Nice bit of work, when it works. Janey wanted it fawn-coloured, to make it look medieval, but I said no: It would have been blood red in Malory's day. That's the thing about medieval dyes....

ROSSETTI   Yes, yes. Come on. You're late.

MORRIS   Perhaps Swinburne would be better. I don't believe, you know.

ROSSETTI   No, you're exactly right.

MORRIS   Don't you think she would have spoken by now, if she'd wanted to?

ROSSETTI   I see her, you know. Every night.

MORRIS   It's just the drug. It's just the filthy drug.

ROSSETTI   I tell you I see her.

MORRIS   How could you not, surrounded by this? Put it away. Paint from life, for a change.

ROSSETTI   What, Fanny?

MORRIS   Yes, even Fanny, if you must. Anyone. Forgive me if this sounds clumsy or rough or wrong, but please — listen. Life is not empty, nor is it made for nothing. And all the parts of it fit into one another in some way. Whether we wish it or not, the world goes on. The world goes on: Beautiful and strange and dreadful and worshipful.

ROSSETTI   I wasn't with Fanny that night, you know. I don't care what anyone says. I went to the College.

MORRIS   Howell said it was closed.

ROSSETTI   Just listen: I went to the College. It was closed. I came home. That's the simple truth. I don't care what Howell says. I didn't see Fanny. I didn't see Fanny because she wasn't there. That's why I came home. Home by eleven. Home *at* eleven.

MORRIS   Howell said half past. But, yes, how could you know, how could anyone know Lizzie would —

ROSSETTI   Exactly. How could I know? I undressed. I went to bed, and she was there, face down... and then she started to snore. And when I tried to turn her over, on to her back, I pricked my thumb on the pin on the note —

MORRIS   So, there was a note?

ROSSETTI   Howell made me burn it. He said we had to.

MORRIS   And what did it say?

ROSSETTI   I don't know. I don't remember. I don't know.

Act II, Scene 3

ROSSETTI's inner monologue.

ROSSETTI   I came home. I undressed. I went to bed, and she was there, face down, looking lovely. I thought... I thought she was... that she wanted to pretend.... And she was so lovely. So innocent — her night-gown pulled up, her hair like a fan. Thick and heavy and bright. Too proud to ask, of course. I thought: Yes. Let's pretend, then.... And after... after she started to snore... when I tried to turn her over, on to her back, I pricked my thumb on the pin on the note. And that's when I knew she wasn't sleeping... or proud... or pretending.... She was dying.

Act II, Scene 4

Return to previous scene.

ROSSETTI   Howell says we have to do it tonight. On her birthday. In her birth hour. Now.

ROSSETTI *and* MORRIS *start séance.*

Hand on hand. Breathe in. Breathe out. Breathe in. Breathe out.... Do you see anything?

MORRIS   Nice table! Elm, isn't it? Oh, woodworm. Too bad. Too bad.

ROSSETTI	Topsy! You're breaking the mood! Hand on hand! Hand on hand! If there's a spirit here who knows us: One for "yes," two for "no."
MORRIS	*(correcting him)* Two for "yes," one for "no."

> SIDDAL's *ghost, sitting on table, knocks once.*

ROSSETTI	Yes!
MORRIS	Or no! Try again.
ROSSETTI	Is it one knock for "yes?"

> SIDDAL *knocks twice.*

MORRIS	*(to* ROSSETTI) Does that mean "no" or "yes"...? Or is the spirit telling us the correct number of knocks for the answer, if the answer is "yes"?
ROSSETTI	Topsy, please.
MORRIS	Let's begin again. Is the year 1869?

> SIDDAL *knocks twice.*

Good. Two knocks for "yes." Now, is there a spirit in the room friendly to either one of us?

> SIDDAL *knocks twice.*

And are your initials E.R?

> SIDDAL *knocks once.*

ROSSETTI	E.S?

> SIDDAL *is silent.*

MORRIS	Who are you?

> SIDDAL *knocks five times, then two more.*

ROSSETTI   F!

MORRIS   G!

ROSSETTI   G — is it you, Papa?

MORRIS   G....

ROSSETTI   Guggum! Is it my little Guggum?

> SIDDAL *knocks twice.*

It is! I knew it! Sweetness. Dearest Dove Divine. Hulloa! Happy Birthday! Do you remember the very last thing I gave you? The little book. The little grey-green book with all my poems?

> SIDDAL *knocks twice.*

Do you have it there with you?

> SIDDAL *knocks twice.*

Excellent. Now. The poem "Jenny." You remember that poem, don't you? *(said quickly, just to refresh SIDDAL's memory)* "Lazy laughing languid Jenny, fond of a kiss and fond of a guinea, whose head upon my knee tonight, rests for a while as if grown light...?"

> SIDDAL *is furious. Knocks twice.*

Good. Now, Lizzie. The seventh stanza:

"Well, handsome Fanny mine, sit up
I've filled our glasses, let us sup
And do not...."

Now, is it "...let *me* think of you...."?

> SIDDAL *knocks twice.*

Good.

"And do not let me think of you
lest...."

Lest what? Lizzie. Can you tell me? Can you tell
me lest what?

> SIDDAL *knocks three times.*

Three! What does that mean?

MORRIS   I think it might mean "perhaps."

ROSSETTI   If I were to hold a paper and pen, would you
write out "Jenny" for me? Would you do that,
dearest little dove?

> SIDDAL *shakes the table furiously.*

Good! Good girl.

> ROSSETTI *waits for automatic writing
> to begin.*

SIDDAL   "Lazy, Filthy, Stinking Fanny
Greasy, Poxied Slut from Hell...."

ROSSETTI   Nothing! Damn me. What now?

MORRIS   What will you do?

ROSSETTI   What can I do? I need "Jenny."

MORRIS   I thought your friends had copies.

ROSSETTI   *(bitterly, pointedly)* I thought so, too. I need the
poem. I need it. I need the poem.

MORRIS   Try writing it again. It might come back to you.
The way the sonnet came back in Italy.

ROSSETTI   It didn't. Not all of it.

MORRIS   Perhaps it will, though, this time. What else can
you do? Begin again. Try to dream it back.

ROSSETTI   Do you think so?

>   SIDDAL *knocks three times.*

SIDDAL   No. No. No.

>   SIDDAL *remains onstage until she
makes the choice to leave* ROSSETTI
in the penultimate scene of the play.

Act II, Scene 5

>   *November, 1869.* ROSSETTI's *studio.*

ROSSETTI   *(to* MORRIS*)* Ah. You've heard.

MORRIS   Everyone's heard.

ROSSETTI   I suppose Janey told you?

MORRIS   Howell.

ROSSETTI   And I suppose you blame me.

MORRIS   No one who knows you blames you. Art isn't
meant to be left in a hole.

ROSSETTI   It was horrible — horrible — the smell —

MORRIS   Lizzie?

ROSSETTI	Oh, not her — no. The disinfectant for the book. She looked beautiful as always, completely unchanged. Her lovely hair had grown, grown to fill the coffin with its gold.
MORRIS	Surely not. Not after seven years.
ROSSETTI	Can't you even leave me with that?
MORRIS	Very well. If you say she was unchanged —
ROSSETTI	She was as perfect as when we laid her in her grave, Howell said.
MORRIS	Ah. Howell... Howell. So, you didn't go?
ROSSETTI	No. We thought it best. My nerves. It wasn't just Lizzie. Aunt Margaret was on top.
MORRIS	And was it worth it?
ROSSETTI	Yes. Almost. "Dante at Verona" is as good as I thought. "The Bride's Chamber" not quite. But poor "Jenny"....
MORRIS	What about "Jenny?"
ROSSETTI	Gone.
MORRIS	Gone? How?
ROSSETTI	A moth, perhaps — Howell said perhaps a butterfly — whatever it was, there's a hole straight through the middle....
SIDDAL	"Oh, Rose, thou art sick...."
ROSSETTI	Through all the parts I most wanted.
SIDDAL	"The invisible worm that flies through the night...."

MORRIS	What are you going to do?
ROSSETTI	What can I do?
MORRIS	Begin again. Try to dream "Jenny" back.
SIDDAL	"Does thy life destroy...."
MORRIS	Is it *that* important?
ROSSETTI	Yes.

Act II, Scene 6

There has been a passage of time.

ROSSETTI *reads.*

ROSSETTI "Lazy, laughing, languid Jenny
Fond of a kiss and fond of a guinea
Whose head upon my knee tonight
Rests for a while, as if grown light
With all our dances and the sound
To which the wild tunes spun you round:
Fair Jenny mine, the thoughtless queen
Of kisses which the blush between
Could hardly make much daintier;
Whose eyes are as blue skies, whose hair
Is countless gold incomparable
Fresh flower, scarce touched with signs that tell
Of Love's exuberant hotbed — Nay,
Poor flower left torn since yesterday
Until to-morrow leave you bare:
Poor handful of bright spring-water
Flung in the whirlpool's shrieking face
Poor shameful Jenny, full of grace
Thus with your head upon my knee
Whose person or whose purse may be
The lodestar of your reverie?

ROSSETTI	*(to* MORRIS*)* Clever, isn't it?
MORRIS	Very. "Clever as paint...."

> ROSSETTI *laughs, recognizing the saying.*

ROSSETTI	"And twice as nourishing...."
SIDDAL	Too clever by half.
ROSSETTI	"Too clever by half," poor Lizzie would have said.
MORRIS	She'd be right.
ROSSETTI	The reviewers will hate it, of course.
MORRIS	I think it's lovely.
ROSSETTI	So you'll review it?
MORRIS	It would hardly be fair.
ROSSETTI	If you review now, it will stop the worst of the rumours. What a pity we don't have our own press.
MORRIS	What a splendid idea. I think that's splendid! We could do Chaucer.
ROSSETTI	I was thinking of something more contemporary.
MORRIS	Malory. Yes, of course, Malory! Think! Who better than us to do Malory?
ROSSETTI	But we've done it to death. Lizzie and I did it ages ago.
MORRIS	Exactly. Don't you see? We've been living Malory all our lives. And think of it: Our own edition. Our vision of Malory for eternity!

ROSSETTI   Perhaps you're right. I still have some old
            sketches of Janey.

MORRIS   Or we could use Georgie.

ROSSETTI   What! Georgie! For Queen Guenevere! Little
            Georgie Jones! I know you and Georgie are —
            but Georgie!

MORRIS   It would make her so pleased. And we could let
            her do some of the wood-cuts. Perhaps this....

                MORRIS *thumbs through Malory for*
                his favourite quote.

            "And then, as the French book saith, the Queen
            and Launcelot were together. And whether they
            were abed, me list hereof, for love at that time
            was not as is nowadays...." *(repeats it lovingly)*
            "For love at that time was not as is
            nowadays...." Wouldn't that be splendid?

ROSSETTI   Hmm. Wouldn't this be better? *(reads)* "Sir
            Launcelot went unto bed with the Queen, and
            took his pleasance and his liking until it was in
            the dawning of the day...."

MORRIS   I don't think Georgie would approve. She's very
            moral.

                ROSSETTI *thumbs through book.*

ROSSETTI   Then let's do this: "The King had a deming of
            hit, but he wold not here theroff, for Sir
            Launcelot had done so much for hym and for the
            Queen so many times that the King loved hym
            passyingly well...." I've always liked that:
            Arthur knowing, but not wanting to be told. We
            could do some splendid things with that. Janey in
            bed.... Look!

Shows MORRIS *sketches.*

MORRIS   They're very good. That's very nice. Eve?

ROSSETTI   Close. Proserpina.

MORRIS   If she's Proserpina, why is she holding an apple?

ROSSETTI   Shouldn't she be?

MORRIS   No. It's a pomegranate. Apples are original sin.

ROSSETTI   Ah. Half-right, then. I've been writing as well!

> ROSSETTI *hands* MORRIS *a poem about Janey.*

Love poems. Good, aren't they? Janey thinks so.

A loose letter falls.

MORRIS   And what's this?

ROSSETTI   Nothing. By the way, Tops, you haven't found those spectacles of mine, have you? I have a feeling they've got into your room somehow. Perhaps under your bed.

MORRIS   I've been thinking....

ROSSETTI   Yes, and so have I! Our press could bring out the second edition of my poems, and you could review it.... And some of your early work, if you like. Your "Defence of Guenevere" perhaps. And I could do the drawings for you. If I find my spectacles.

MORRIS   Perhaps "The Hollow Land" might be more timely.

ROSSETTI   "The Hollow Land." Bit grim. Any part in particular?

MORRIS	Yes, the end.
ROSSETTI	The end? You mean Florian's death?
MORRIS	No. Florian rising from the ground, encased with the slimy earth and coiling worms of physical decay, might be nice. It's the dead soul in living body I find interesting. Don't you?
ROSSETTI	Less and less.
MORRIS	I keep remembering that line from Lizzie: "Do the dead walk hand in hand...." How does it go?
ROSSETTI	*(not very keen)* "Do the dead walk hand in hand...."
MORRIS	No, what was the rest of it?
ROSSETTI	I don't remember.
MORRIS	You must. "Do the dead walk hand in hand...."
ROSSETTI	"Do we clasp dead hands and quiver With an endless joy forever...."

MORRIS *pretends to see* SIDDAL, *but points somewhere else entirely.*

MORRIS	Oh look! It's Lizzie. I see Lizzie.

SIDDAL *looks in the direction he is pointing.*

ROSSETTI	Where?
MORRIS	Over there. In the corner. I see her. She's trying to say something... it's very faint....
ROSSETTI	Can you make it out?

MORRIS	I think so. Yes. She's saying: "When we... met ourselves." When we met ourselves.... What can that mean?
ROSSETTI	*(frightened)* Is she still there? Has she gone yet?
MORRIS	No. She seems to be holding a letter... in her hand.... And she says she still loves you, even now. It's been seven long years, and she loves you and she wants to be with you forever.

> ROSSETTI *faints, falling into Wallis's "Chatterton" death pose.*

Act II, Scene 7

Moments later.

MORRIS	Gabriel... please... please....
ROSSETTI	*(thinks he's seen a vision)* I dreamed I looked out my window and I saw a crowd, a large crowd, carrying gibbets. Gibbets to hang me on.
MORRIS	*(practical explanation)* They aren't gibbets, they're walking sticks... you must have seen people carrying walking sticks for the Festival.
ROSSETTI	I tell you they were gibbets! They came closer and closer, and a voice not my own — *not* my own — said something. Something terrible.
MORRIS	But what? What could be so terrible? What would anyone have said?
ROSSETTI	About me. About poor Lizzie. A terrible, terrible word.
MORRIS	Adulterer?

ROSSETTI	Worse. Much worse.
MORRIS	Murderer? *(beat)* Grave robber?
SIDDAL	*(ghostly)* Thief.
ROSSETTI	I heard everyone laughing. Laughing at us. Laughing at all of us.
MORRIS	It doesn't matter.
ROSSETTI	Don't you care what they say?
MORRIS	Only the Art matters.
ROSSETTI	I'm not a good man, William. You know that, don't you? I don't deserve your love.
MORRIS	Love isn't earned. Try to sleep. Tomorrow will be better. I promise.

Act II, Scene 8

ROSSETTI*'s guilt dream.*

SIDDAL	"Is this what you'd like? Is this what she does? Is this why you prefer her to me...?"
	"You make me so miserable, I don't care anymore. I want to be dead...."
	"And if it doesn't kill me, let's see what it does to the baby. Shall we see if we can kill this one the way we killed the last...?"
	"Then let me come too...."
	"But why not? Tell me why. Because you're going to *her*, aren't you...?"

ROSSETTI   "No. because I can't stand the smell of you...."

Oh Lizzie, I'm so sorry. I'm so sorry.

> *He measures out his chloral into a glass.*

"My life is so miserable
I wish for no more of it...."

"My life is so miserable
I wish for no more...."

"My life is so miserable...."

SIDDAL   "Thy strong arms are around me, love
My head is on thy breast
Low words of comfort come from thee
Yet my soul has no rest.

For I am but a startled thing
Nor can I ever be
Aught save a bird whose broken wings
Must fly away from thee.

I cannot give to thee the love
I gave so long ago
The love that turned and struck me down
Amid the blinding snow.

I can but give a failing heart
And weary eyes of pain
A faded mouth that cannot smile
And may not smile again.

Yet keep thine arms around me, love
Until I fall asleep
Then leave me, saying no good-bye
Lest I might wake, and weep."

SIDDAL *exits.*

ROSSETTI *wakes.*

ROSSETTI   *(to* SIDDAL*)* Don't leave! I'll die if you leave me. Please.

MORRIS   *(to* ROSSETTI*)* I won't leave. I'll never leave.

Act II, Scene 9

A month later.

Musical bridge from Wagner's "Tristan und Isolde." ROSSETTI *is prosperous, but unwell. Paintings of Janey are everywhere.*

ROSSETTI   *(shaving, calls)* Ah, good. You came. Come through... come through!

MORRIS   Have you finished the sketches already?

ROSSETTI   No. I wanted to give you something! It's a birthday present!

MORRIS   It isn't my birthday.

ROSSETTI   Then it's an *un*birthday present. To celebrate... something. What does it matter? Go on, open it!

MORRIS *opens wrapped book. He reads the title, puzzled.*

MORRIS   "The Moral Force Of Teetotalism...." *(more puzzled)* "Illustrated In The Life Of William Morris...."

ROSSETTI   Yes, I thought you'd be pleased. No relation, I
presume. We found it down Charing Cross Road
the day before last.

MORRIS   And you've kept it all this time!

ROSSETTI   Yes. It was difficult, of course, but you know
how well I can keep a secret when I want to.

MORRIS   It's lovely. You're too generous. Thank you.

ROSSETTI   Thank Janey. She found it. Pass me those
trousers. The ones on the chair.

MORRIS   Which ones?

ROSSETTI   Either will do. Coming with us tonight?

MORRIS   I'm hardly dressed to go to the opera.

ROSSETTI tosses him trousers.

ROSSETTI   Not to worry. Try these on for size.

MORRIS hesitates.

Well, go on.

MORRIS changes trousers.

What's yours is mine, as they say.

MORRIS   Isn't it "What's mine is yours?"

ROSSETTI   Either way. Do they fit?

MORRIS   A little long in the leg, a little tight in the thigh,
and the buttons won't do up.

ROSSETTI   Perfect!

MORRIS   I feel like a bear in a corset. And I *hate* "Tristram
and Isolde."

ROSSETTI   I know, so do I. But Janey loves it. We all make
what sacrifices we can, for Art, my friend. Here.
Let me see what I can do. *(arranges* MORRIS*'s
clothes)* Don't move! Stay just as you are! There!

> *"Tristan und Isolde" music fades into*
> SIDDAL *singing "Oh, Never Weep":*

SIDDAL   "Oh never weep for love that's dead
For love is seldom true
But changes his fashion from blue to red
From brightest red to blue
And love was born to an early grave
And is so seldom true.

Sweet, never weep for what cannot be
For this God has not given.
If the merest dream of love were true
Then sweet, we should be in heaven.
And this is only earth, my dear
Where true love is not given."

> SIDDAL*'s pose echoes* ROSSETTI*'s
> painting "Beata Beatrix."*

ROSSETTI   *(to* MORRIS*)* Stay just as you are. *(beat)*
Perfect!

Suggestions for Further Reading

G.B-J [Georgiana, Lady Burne-Jones]. *Memorials of Edward Burne-Jones*. London: Macmillan, 1904.

John Bryson (editor), with Introduction by John Bryson in association with Janet Camp Troxell, *Dante Gabriel Rossetti and Jane Morris: Their Correspondence*. Oxford: Clarendon, 1976.

Paull Franklin Baum (editor), *Dante Gabriel Rossetti's Letters to Fanny Cornforth*. Baltimore: Johns Hopkins Press, 1940.

W.R. Crump (editor), *The Complete Poems of Christina Rossetti*, three volumes, Louisiana University Press, 1979-1990.

Walter H. Godfrey, *The Survey of London*. Issued by the Joint Publishing Committee representing the London County Council and the Committee for the Survey of the Memorials of Greater London, Vol. 2, The Parish of Chelsea, Part 1, 1909.

Violet Hunt, *The Wife of Rossetti*. London: John Lane, 1932.

Jan Marsh, *Elizabeth Siddal, 1829-1862: Pre-Raphaelite Artist*. Sheffield: Sheffield Arts Department, 1991.

Jan Marsh, *Jane and May Morris: A Biographical Story, 1839-1938*. London: Pandora, 1986.

Jan Marsh, *The Legend of Elizabeth Siddal*. London: Quartet, 1989.

Jan Marsh, *The Pre-Raphaelite Sisterhood*. London: Quartet, 1985.

Fiona McCarthy, *William Morris*. London: Faber, 1994.

David Rodgers, *William Morris at Home*. London: Ebury, 1996.

Evelyn Waugh, *Rossetti: His Life and Works*. London: Duckworth, 1928.

The Ash Grove — Welsh Traditional.

poignantly.

Down yonder green val-ley where streamlets me-an-der where
twi-light is fad-ing I pen-sive-ly rove. Or
at the bright moon-tide In sol-i-tude wan-der A-
-mid the dark shades of the lone-ly ash-grove with
sor-row deep sor-row My bos-om is
lad-en. All day I go a-mourn-ing In search of my

love: ye echoes. Oh tell me where is the sweet

maid-en? She sleeps 'neath the green turf Down

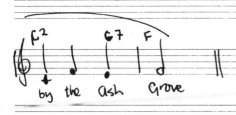

by the ash Grove

Refrain from "Early one morning" (Trad.) arranged Elizabeth Parker

Oh, don't de-ceive me. Oh, nev-er leave me.

How could you treat a poor maiden so?